THE Boys' Guide TO
GROWTH MINDSET

THE Boys' Guide TO
GROWTH MINDSET

A Can-Do Approach to Building
Confidence, Resilience, and Courage

OLUWATOSIN AKINDELE, LMSW

ROCKRIDGE
PRESS

FOR AIDEN JAMES, LINAIYA REIGN, AND ASHA ELISE—
THANK YOU FOR INSPIRING ME DAILY AND SHOWING ME
THAT NOTHING IS IMPOSSIBLE. I LOVE YOU.

First Rockridge Press trade paperback edition 2022

Rockridge Press and the Rockridge Press logo are trademarks or registered trademarks of Callisto Media Inc. and/or its affiliates in the United States and other countries and may not be used without written permission.

For general information on our other products and services, please contact our Customer Care Department within the United States at (866) 744-2665, or outside the United States at (510) 253-0500.

Paperback ISBN: 978-1-68539-900-9 | eBook ISBN: 978-1-68539-331-1

Manufactured in the United States of America

Series Designer: Jennifer Hsu
Interior and Cover Designer: Irene Vandervoort
Art Producer: Melissa Malinowsky
Editor: Julie Haverkate
Production Editor: Jael Fogle
Production Manager: Jose Olivera

Illustrations © softulka/Creative Market, pp. ii, vi, 4, 7, 10, 11, 13, 15, 17, 24, 30, 33, 50, 51, 62, 65, 74, 91, 140; istock, pp. 30, 31, 84, 85, 121; © Ale Estrada/The Noun Project, p. 96; All other illustrations used under license from Shutterstock.com; Author photo courtesy of Erica Mathlin

10 9 8 7 6 5 4 3 2 1 0

CONTENTS

CONTENTS

INTRODUCTION

Your voice, feelings, thoughts, and emotions matter. *You* matter. You have the power to think big and dream bigger. My name is Tosin, and every day I work with boys just like you to unlock this power. As a therapist, I help kids recognize their own strengths and build confidence. Whether or not you have heard of growth mindset, you have already used it before. Just think about all the times you've pushed yourself to try something new or the times you've worked to make something better. These are parts of growth mindset, and you're about to discover so much more.

All the tools you need to be as happy and successful as possible are right here at your fingertips. This book is a map to guide you through any obstacles and difficulties you face. You will learn how to set goals, take risks, embrace challenges, and improve your relationships with family, friends, and teachers. As you go through life, you will transition through different schools and communities. There will be many experiences that shape who you are. Some will seem hard or even impossible to deal with. But with practice, you will develop all the skills you need to face anything. Let's get to know who you are and who you can be.

How to Use This Book

There is no right or wrong way to explore this book. All I ask is that you have an open mind and take your time. You are going to be introduced to plenty of new ideas, but don't be overwhelmed. The book is divided into different chapters that let you soak everything in at your own pace. There are plenty of exercises, activities, and games in each section that will help you practice growth mindset skills. Have fun with these! Your brain is always more likely to retain information that you are excited about. The more time you put into practicing these skills, the more you will get out of them.

As you go through the book, feel free to skip ahead to different sections that you find most relevant or interesting. Do the

exercises in any order you choose. You can always refer back to earlier chapters if you need more clarity or more practice. Feel free to share your thoughts with a trusted friend or family member. Ask them questions! Everyone in your life has had their own experiences with learning, making mistakes, and trying again. They'll have lots of good insight to inspire you as you set your own goals and discover your own path of growth.

Think of this book as a safe space. It is not a textbook, and you will not be tested at the end. Be kind to yourself as you try new things and discover different ways of tackling challenges. Remember that no one is perfect the first time around. So grab a pencil or pen, put on your creativity cap, and let's roll!

I CAN
LEARN
TO DO
ANYTHING

CHAPTER ONE

WHAT IS A GROWTH MINDSET?

As you continue to grow, so does your brain. It changes in exciting ways and has limitless potential to learn. Since the age of two, your brain has been developing connections through everyday experiences. These connections have been shaped by your environment. At your present age, you are now able to tell the difference between something that's very hard and something that is not very hard. This is typically when you start showing characteristics of growth mindsets and fixed mindsets.

Growth Mindsets versus Fixed Mindsets

Growth mindset is believing in yourself and your ability to overcome challenges. Have you ever seen a toddler try to do something that they can't yet do on their own, like walk or climb? After trying and failing, do they quit, or do they keep trying? I've never seen a toddler want something and give up without being assisted by an adult. This dedication and persistence are part of a growth mindset.

The opposite of a growth mindset is a fixed mindset. When you have a fixed mindset, you believe that skills are things you are born with. If you are not good at something, your fixed mindset thinks you will never be good at it, no matter how much work you put in. Here are a few examples:

Growth mindset: I appreciate and welcome **feedback** because it helps me learn and grow.

Fixed mindset: When I receive feedback, it feels like disapproval.

Growth mindset: Learning to skate is tricky, but I know I will get better.

Fixed mindset: Some people are just naturally good skaters. I'll never be like them.

Growth mindset: There is always room for improvement.

Fixed mindset: I'm already a really good writer. I don't need to get any better.

TRY THIS! MY MINDSET

Circle the example in each row that best describes you. It's important to be honest. If your responses lean toward a fixed mindset, don't worry. This is normal! Everyone has areas where they'll fit the growth mindset and areas where they'll fit the fixed mindset.

GROWTH MINDSET	FIXED MINDSET
I see failures as opportunities for growth.	If I don't try, then I won't fail.
I can learn to do anything.	I'm either good at something or not.
I'm inspired by other people's success.	I'm jealous of other people's success.
When I'm frustrated, I keep trying.	When I'm frustrated, I give up.
I enjoy trying new things.	I only stick to what I know.
I ask for help when I need it.	I avoid asking for help because people may think I don't know how to do something.
When I don't succeed at first, I give it another shot.	If I don't succeed immediately, it's time to try something else.

Studying the Growth Mindset

Over thirty years ago, psychologist Dr. Carol Dweck developed the concept of growth mindset. Her research found that there is power in believing you can do something. She described how beliefs influence what people want and whether they are successful in achieving those things. Dweck's work shows that people who have a growth mindset see challenges as ways to improve. They are often better prepared to face problems and learn from them.

Think about a time you wanted to do something without realizing how difficult it was. Your first instinct might have been to stop. But if you kept going and tried to find ways around the challenge, you were showing a growth mindset. Dweck says that a growth mindset is essential for success. The good news is that growth mindset skills can be learned. You've already started developing these skills by reading this book!

Principles of a Growth Mindset

A growth mindset isn't defined as just one thing. Following are some of the principles that combine to make a growth mindset.

* **Effort and hard work are the keys to success, not just talent.** Everyone is talented at something. You still need to work hard to strengthen and further improve upon that talent to get the most out of it.

* **Mistakes and failures help you learn.** We all make mistakes—no one is perfect. What's important is learning from mistakes and trying not to repeat them.

* **You can create positive thoughts.** When unhelpful thoughts creep in, you can **reframe** them. This is a way to push out negativity. For example, "I knew that assignment was going to be too hard for me; I should not have tried!" can be reframed as "That assignment was really tough, but I'll be better prepared next time."

* **Frustration is a normal part of growth.** The fact that you get frustrated when you make mistakes shows that you care. The next time you fail at something and experience frustration, allow yourself the time and space to feel it. Then start to think of different ways you could make improvements.

* **Feedback and criticism are important for change.** Taking feedback can be difficult. Just remember that when people give feedback, it's because they want to see you succeed.

Let's practice reframing unhelpful thoughts. Reframing is when you actively notice unhelpful thoughts in your mind and change them into more useful thoughts. It's like how remixing a song can put a new spin on it.

Draw a line from each unhelpful thought to its reframed form. In the empty spaces at the bottom, write an unhelpful thought that has crossed your mind. Then try reframing it! The more you practice reframing your unhelpful thoughts, the less they will have a negative impact.

Unhelpful Thought	Reframed Thought
I always make silly mistakes!	Being forgetful sometimes doesn't make me a bad friend.
I forgot my friend's birthday. I am the worst friend ever.	I can avoid mistakes in the future by being more careful.
I flunked this test because I am terrible at science.	I can do better on my next test by studying more.

Discovering Your Passions

When you have passion for something, you really care about it. Think about someone you admire. It could be anyone—a professional athlete, a world-class gamer, or your local Scout leader who organizes cool activities. The fact that you can identify them means you recognize their hard work. Their passion has led to success. Developing a growth mindset can help you discover your passions and put you on a similar path to success.

Being disciplined to work for many, many hours is an act of passion. The person you admire didn't become successful overnight. They had to start somewhere, and they had to use a growth mindset to keep at it. Think about how you approach the things you are passionate about. How does that passion translate? For example, if you are passionate about singing or rapping, that passion can encourage you to learn how to play an instrument or produce beats. A growth mindset allows you to branch out and embrace new things, even if you struggle with them at first. This can open you up to all sorts of exciting new experiences.

GROWTH MINDSET
IN ACTION

JEREMY LIN was born in Torrance, California, in 1988 to Taiwanese immigrants. Throughout his basketball career, Jeremy had to fight to earn his spot on every team he has been on. He played college basketball at Harvard University as a walk-on, meaning he was not given an athletic scholarship. When Jeremy joined the Golden State Warriors as an undrafted player in 2010, he did not see much playing time. It was not until he was traded to the New York Knicks in 2012 that he was given an opportunity to play. Jeremy snatched this opportunity and made the most of it, going on to set records. As of 2021, Jeremy has played for nine NBA teams and seven different teams since his historic run with the New York Knicks in 2012. He never allowed this inconsistency to distract or defeat him. Jeremy used a growth mindset to persevere through constant change, always helping whatever team he was on to the best of his ability.

TRY THIS! CREATE A VISION BOARD

Vision boards are a way to lay out your interests and motivate you to explore them. They are typically created with photos, drawings, cutouts from magazines, or even words and phrases. Make your own vision board in the following space. Find or draw images and words that represent an activity you enjoy. Whenever you need inspiration or motivation, refer to this visual collection.

What Are Your Superpowers?

Superpowers aren't just seen in comic books and superhero movies. Did you know you have your very own superpowers? These are your unique strengths and abilities. Anything that you are really good at is a superpower. It could be your positive attitude or reading skills that are above grade level. Just like a superhero, you can use your powers to face challenges and solve problems. Are you a kind person? If so, then that can be one of your superpowers! Kindness allows you to make others smile by helping them and lifting their moods. But it's also something that can get you through difficult times. For example, when you try to do something and it doesn't quite work out the way you want it to, use your kindness superpowers. Instead of getting down on yourself, be kind by reassuring yourself that you will do better next time.

Everyone has superpowers! Find and circle the ten differ-ent powers in the word search. Then check off any that relate to you.

C S T U S C D A W L
U A D V E N T U R E
R A T H L E T I C S
I N H E W B R O H M
O Z U G I R E G O U
S L M T S A A A N S
I J O R D V D M E I
T N R B O E I E S C
Y V D A M R N S T B
I F M Z G Y G B Y J

☐ adventure   ☐ games   ☐ music
☐ athletics   ☐ honesty   ☐ reading
☐ bravery   ☐ humor   ☐ wisdom
☐ curiosity

Keep Going!

Can you think of something you started that became more difficult as you progressed? In situations like this, there are usually two ways you can go. You show a fixed mindset by giving up, or you find a way to continue and push through with a growth mindset. Pushing through and sticking with something is called **perseverance**. You persevere when you keep doing something even when obstacles arise. Even though it can be difficult, we can all practice perseverance and get better at it. Have you ever tried to solve a tricky math problem and got it wrong? In that situation, perseverance would be trying a different method to solve the equation without giving up.

There is a level of excitement and sense of accomplishment that only comes from completing a difficult task. Of course, this is easier said than done. New challenges can be very scary and intimidating. The best way to tackle any obstacle is to keep your desired results in mind. **Visualize** the outcome you want. Let's say you're at the skate park and want to try some new tricks on the ramp. Rather than fearing the steepness of the ramp, picture yourself landing the trick.

Let's get to know different types of perseverance. Read each scenario, and then circle the response that shows perseverance. It's okay if you don't choose the correct response. This is a learning process, and there's still so much more to learn!

1. You slipped up in basketball, and your team lost the game. You:

    a. Decide you're just not good at basketball, so you quit.

    b. Spend more time practicing with your coach and teammates.

2. In rehearsals for the school play, you keep forgetting your lines. You:

    a. Tell the director that you can't do it.

    b. Spend extra time memorizing your lines.

3. You missed your bus and were late to school. You:

    a. Try to leave home a little earlier in the mornings.

    b. Get upset and blame yourself for not being a morning person.

Answers: 1: b; 2: b; 3: a

The Benefits of a Growth Mindset

Having a growth mindset can help you in all parts of your life, whether it's at school, at home, or in your hobbies. For example, it can motivate you to develop strong study habits, which will improve your grades at school.

No matter how good you are at something, there is always a way to improve. Perseverance is useful when you're learning a new skill. We learn new things every day. New skills can sometimes be challenging, but perseverance will keep you from quitting. Challenge yourself to continue looking for ways to get better. Once you've adopted a growth mindset, you'll start to look at challenges in a different light. They will no longer be roadblocks but puzzles to find new ways to succeed. It also means you'll have way more fun! If you struggle with growth mindset today, tomorrow is a brand-new day to work on it.

I CAN
HELP
MY BRAIN GET
STRONGER

CHAPTER TWO
YOUR AMAZING BRAIN!

Your brain will not be fully formed until you are twenty-five years old. Even then, it will continue to adapt and change. Amazing, right? In fact, the reason we can keep learning new skills at any age is because of our incredible and complex brain. In this chapter, we will take a look inside your head to see how it all works. You'll discover the different parts of the brain and find out what they do. We'll continue exploring growth mindset along the way and how the brain can be used to assist your mindset.

Your Brain at Work

The brain is an organ that controls everything your body does, from talking to waving to breathing. It is also responsible for things other than physical actions, like our thoughts, memories, and emotions.

Brains are a major part of the **nervous system**. This is a vast network that contains trillions of nerves throughout the entire human body. The nerves send signals to the brain, and the brain tells your body how to respond. When you touch something hot or smell something delicious, that information travels through the nerves to your brain. In short, the brain is like a computer that processes information and controls body functions. The nervous system relays the information to different parts of the body.

Your brain continues to learn things for as long as you live. This is possible through a process called **neuroplasticity**. Although that's a big word, it is simply the brain's ability to grow and change over time. If you ever learned to ride a bike, you probably remember how hard it was the first time. It may have even felt scary. But you eventually got there by practice. Like any muscle in your body, the brain gets stronger the more you use it. This also explains how practicing to do something leads your brain to figure out how to do it. That's why it's important to persevere at things, even if they're difficult at first. You're training your brain!

The Parts of the Brain

The brain is made up of different parts with their own special functions. Check out what the parts do and how they work.

Cerebrum: This is the largest part of your brain. It controls your thoughts, movements, and memory. What did you have for dinner last night? Who was your kindergarten teacher? Your **cerebrum** is the reason you are able to answer those questions.

Cerebellum: Notice how you use your hands and fingers to turn these pages. The precision in those movements comes from your **cerebellum**. This part of your brain also controls your balance. When you sit, your cerebellum helps you stay upright.

Brain stem: Place your hand over your heart. Do you feel that beating? Your **brain stem** is responsible for things you do automatically, like your heartbeat, breathing, digesting food, and sneezing. Reflexes are also controlled by your brain stem. Your reflexes go into action when you drop something and catch it before it hits the ground. The brain stem connects your brain to the **spinal cord**.

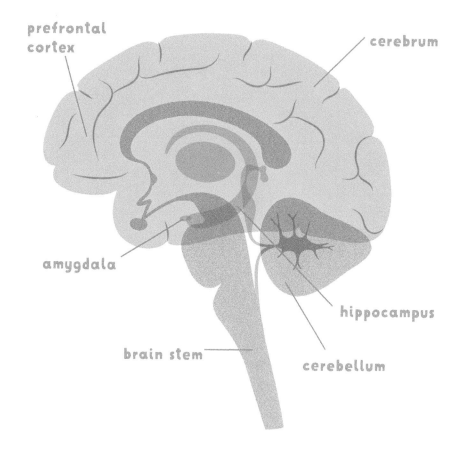

prefrontal cortex

cerebrum

amygdala

hippocampus

brain stem

cerebellum

Amygdala: The main job of the **amygdala** is to regulate and process emotions. It presents you with the option to fight, freeze, run, or faint when you are in a scary situation. It also plays a primary role in decision-making. When you have a fixed mindset, it may be your amygdala making it hard for you to accept new challenges. This is because it is trying to keep you safe by responding with fear. The amygdala controls your ability to respond to danger and survive.

Prefrontal cortex: This part of the brain is responsible for choices, planning, and self-control. What you choose to wear, have for lunch, and how you plan your day are all things that are managed by your **prefrontal cortex**. The prefrontal cortex is essential to growth mindset because it helps you take risks. You don't need to worry about failure because your prefrontal cortex will help you navigate past all challenges.

Improving your memory will help you stretch and build a healthy brain. Try it now! Take a look around your kitchen, and then go to another room. Now map out the kitchen in the space below. Try to remember the location of appliances and furniture, the number of cabinets and drawers, and the color of everything. Be as detailed as you can. When you've finished, go back to the kitchen and check your drawing. What did you remember correctly? What did you miss? Go back and make any necessary revisions. Repeat until you've created a strong memory of your kitchen.

Neurons and Pathways

The human body is made up of trillions of **cells**. The cells that work with the nervous system are called **neurons**. Neurons carry messages from different parts of the body to your brain and back. They do this by "talking" with electrical signals that are triggered by their chemicals. But how does the information go from one place to another? It travels through **neural pathways**. Think of these pathways as bridges that connect different parts of the nervous system. As these pathways get stronger, they expand into networks.

When cells divide to create neurons, the process is called **neurogenesis**. You went through the process of neurogenesis before you were even born. As a baby, your brain created many, many neurons—more than you will ever need in your lifetime. This is a good thing because neurons create opportunities to grow and learn. It's like having a big set of colored pencils. It's unlikely you will use every pencil when you create a single drawing, but you want to have all of them available in case you ever need to use them.

The Building Blocks of a Strong Brain

Neurons can boost your ability to learn, keep your mind sharp, and reduce **anxiety**. Luckily, there are many different ways you can gain more of these brain cells—and they're all really fun!

Here are some things you can do to build a stronger brain and keep growing neurons.

* **Do "mental gymnastics."** These can include reading, word puzzles, number games, and building things with toy blocks.

* **Get lots of physical exercise if you can safely do so.** Activities like running, cycling, and swimming are effective ways of boosting neurons.

* **Get outside!** The sun provides vitamin D, which helps produce a lot of the cells needed for neurogenesis. Just make sure you always wear sunscreen.

* **We are what we eat.** Without the right nutrients, it is very difficult for neurogenesis to take place. Healthy food will help that process.

* **Meditate.** Yoga or breathing exercises can help decrease stress, anxiety, and depression. These are all factors that can restrict the growth of new neurons.

So what's the best thing you can do to make your brain grow? Make mistakes! Weird but true. Your brain becomes super active whenever you make them and even lights up. See that? Even your brain wants you to work toward a growth mindset!

You're probably familiar with the benefits of exercise. We usually think of stronger muscles, increased energy, better sleep, and a healthier heart. These are all true, but physical activities also affect one of the most important organs of our bodies. You guessed it: the brain!

A fast-beating heart can promote the growth of neurons and strengthen your brain. As an added bonus, it only takes between ten and thirty minutes of movement every day to lift your mood. Try it right now with this super simple exercise.

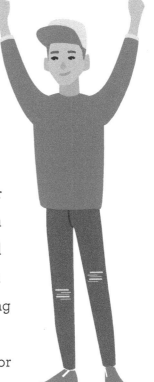

Set a timer for ten minutes and do jumping jacks or arm jacks (bend elbows at a ninety-degree angle with palms facing each other and pump arms up and down). You can put on your favorite music and keep your pace with the beat. Soon enough, you'll get that heart beating fast! If you're up for an extra challenge, see if you can go for fifteen or twenty minutes.

GROWTH MINDSET
IN ACTION

SHAWN "JAY-Z" CARTER is widely regarded as one of the most successful musicians in the world. During the beginning of his career, his success was not guaranteed. In fact, he had to lean heavily into his growth mindset and persevere through many roadblocks on his way to success. One major roadblock Jay-Z faced was when he was turned down by several major record labels. Jay-Z and two of his friends decided that the only way they were going to get his music out was by doing it themselves. They created Roc-A-Fella records in 1995. In 1996, Jay-Z released his critically acclaimed *Reasonable Doubt* album. It went on to sell more than ten million copies. Jay-Z had a growth mindset and did everything in his power to achieve his dreams.

Healthy Brain Habits

Developing and maintaining good brain health will help you have a long and happy life. One of the first things you can do is get into good habits. Habits are hard to break, so the sooner you build good ones, the easier it is to keep them and stay healthy.

Rest

Did you know that your brain is active when you're sleeping? Even when you're asleep, your brain stays wide awake. Sleep is important for successful brain functions, including how your neurons communicate with one another. While you're asleep, **toxins** are removed from your brain to keep it working at its best.

Water and Nutrients

Drinking lots of water and eating nutrient-rich foods can have a positive effect on your brain health. Kids who drink water consistently perform better in activities that require them to think and respond fast, like tests or games. It helps you focus!

⚡ TRY THIS! BUILD A HEALTHY PLATE ⚡

Here are some of the best known "brain foods." Pick an item from each category and create a meal you'd love to eat! Be sure to consider any allergies you have and choose the foods that work best for you.

Best Brain Fruits

* Blueberries support memory and the ability of your brain to function properly.

* Avocados are packed with nutrients that can produce energy in the brain.

Best Brain Veggies

* Asparagus is a great source of nutrition to support focus and learning.

* Broccoli, kale, and cauliflower are rich in chemicals that help rebuild damaged brain cells.

* Beets boost the flow of blood to the front part of your brain.

Best Nuts, Seeds, and Healthy Oils

* Walnuts, pumpkin seeds, chia seeds, and olive oil contain healthy fats that are used for brain energy.

Best Animal Products

* Salmon has healthy fats that help produce brain cells.

* Grass-fed red meat has acids that improve brain function.

* Eggs have nutrients that help with memory.

Exercise

Physical exercise is great for a healthy body and brain. It helps grow new connections between brain cells as well as improve your mood. But there are also mental exercises that benefit our brains. Activities like puzzles and memory games can improve your memory, focus, and creativity.

Unplug

We all have screens that we use for various things: games, reading, watching shows, or talking to loved ones. These are all part of everyday life, but it helps to unplug from these devices. That means limiting your time in front of screens. People who spend less than two hours a day on screen activities tend to score higher on language and thinking tests.

TRY THIS! COUNTING ZZZ'S

When you regularly get a good night's rest, you're likely to have improved attention, behavior, memory, and overall mental and physical health. You should be getting nine to twelve hours of sleep a night. If you struggle with falling asleep or staying asleep, try these tips and tricks.

- ☐ Dim the lights.

- ☐ Take a warm bath before bedtime. Add some **Epsom salts** for added relaxation!

- ☐ Set an alarm to remind you to wind down before you go to bed.

- ☐ Avoid screens or electronic devices an hour before your bedtime.

- ☐ Relax with a quiet, screen-free activity such as reading a book.

- ☐ Do a peaceful mind exercise, like counting backward from one hundred.

- ☐ Breathe slowly and deeply. Inhale for four beats, pause for four beats, exhale for four beats, and hold for four beats. Repeat.

I CAN REFRAME MY THOUGHTS

THE "MIND" IN MINDSET

CHAPTER THREE
THE "MIND" IN MINDSET

Your mind and brain both grow and expand, but they're not the same. The brain is a physical thing that can be touched—it's unlikely you'll ever do so, though, unless you become a doctor! The mind, on the other hand, can't be touched. The mind is your thoughts and understanding of the world around you.

What Are You Thinking?

Thoughts are ideas, opinions, and beliefs you have. As you read these words, the voice you hear inside your head is also part of your thoughts. Have you ever watched a scary movie, and after it was over you were too terrified to sleep? In your mind, you can still hear the sounds and see the images from the movie. Even though your brain knows that the movie was not real and the things in the movie are not going to happen to you, your imagination makes you feel otherwise. It creates an emotional response. We are not our thoughts. Those thoughts only become real when we choose to act on them. So, even though the movie scared you, you can still go to sleep as you would any other night. That's you choosing not to act on your thoughts.

What Is Mindfulness?

Mindfulness is being aware of what you're sensing and thinking in the moment. The key to practicing mindfulness is focusing on yourself. Try to notice any thoughts you are having without judging them. Notice any sensations you are feeling. Being curious about your thoughts and feelings allows you to explore ways to change them.

One way to be mindful is by taking a few deep breaths. Notice each thought that comes and goes like trees outside the window of a moving car. There are times you may not be able to identify how you are feeling or why. When this happens, turn your attention to the sensations in your body. Notice your heartbeat and your posture. Are you clenching your jaw or holding your breath? These might be signs of anxiety or nervousness. This is your invitation to loosen your jaw and breathe slowly. Your body will always tell you whether you are relaxed or uncomfortable. You just have to become familiar with the signs.

Simple mindfulness activities nurture growth mindset because you can notice negative thoughts and reframe them. Being aware of your thoughts and feelings helps you make positive, well-informed decisions.

TRY THIS! FIVE SENSES

A simple way to be mindful is to use all your **senses**. This will bring your attention to the present moment and help you focus. To begin, pick up any object you can hold in your hand. Sit down in a comfortable position and gently close your eyes. Feel every part of the object with your fingers. Explore its shape, material, weight, and texture. Notice how it feels in your hands using your sense of touch. Now open your eyes and use your sight. How does the object look? What colors do you see? Can you use your sense of smell with this object? Think about its scent. Does your sense of hearing notice any sound it makes? If the object is a food, what does it taste like? Take a few minutes to focus on the object and your senses.

The Mind and the Body

Sometimes we get caught up in our thoughts and feelings. When this happens, we can bring awareness to our body and breath to slow down the mind. Being aware will give you the opportunity to use any coping skill you may need in the moment. Mindfulness practices like slow breathing and **meditation** are examples of coping skills. They help recenter your attention to the present as opposed to allowing your mind to wander. Thoughts and feelings come and go, but your breathing is always with you in the present. Focusing on your experience in the present moment makes it easier to distinguish the connection between your thoughts and your feelings. Can you remember a time you were really upset? Were you aware of what your body was doing in that moment? Next time you become frustrated or excited, make a mental note of how your body responds to that emotion. If your body is tense or jittery, adjust its response by trying a mindfulness practice.

Pick an emotion and use your face to act it out. Then use your entire body to become that emotion. Notice your posture. What happens to your shoulders? Does your heart rate increase? Try performing different emotions. Some to try are happy, shy, scared, angry, impatient, and frustrated. How does your breathing change from one emotion to the other?

Act out these emotions again, but make an effort to control your breathing this time. Breathe in and out, slowly and deeply. What changes do you notice in your body once you've taken control of your breathing?

GROWTH MINDSET
IN ACTION

In 2009, **BARACK OBAMA** became the forty-fourth president of the United States. Before that, in his 1995 book *Dreams from My Father: A Story of Race and Inheritance*, he wrote about his struggle with his identity as a Black man raised by a white mother and her parents in the absence of his father. Despite this and other challenges he faced growing up as a young Black man, Barack remained focused on achieving his goals. In the third grade, he wrote an essay about what he wanted to be when he grew up, which—spoiler alert—was president. Barack knew he had to work hard to make that dream a reality. During college, he so intensely concentrated on his studies and committed to running three miles a day (to help boost his neurons!) and to fasting on Sundays that his roommate went so far as to call him a "bore." But it was this dedication, persistence, and hard work that propelled him forward to achieving his third-grade dream.

I Think I Can

You know the dialogue that runs inside your head every day? It might include things like giving yourself instructions while you're completing a task or random observations about your environment and the people around you. That is all **self-talk**. There are two kinds: positive self-talk and negative self-talk. When you spill juice and you call yourself clumsy, that is negative self-talk. When you say, "I've got this" before taking on a task, that is positive self-talk. Self-talk is positive when you have helpful thoughts and negative when you have unhelpful thoughts.

Positive Self-Talk

Positive self-talk is all about showing yourself kindness. This is helpful when you are dealing with a tough task or experiencing negative emotions. Positive self-talk helps reframe the way you view challenging or upsetting situations. If you are heading into a difficult task with a positive attitude, you are more likely to succeed. Give the task everything you have. Instead of saying, "Hopefully it will go well," say, "I can do this." Positive self-talk also boosts confidence. It is very inspiring to tell yourself that you're going to give it your best, no matter what happens.

A way to practice positive self-talk is through **affirmations**. These are positive thoughts that you repeat to yourself. When you have an unhelpful thought, respond with an affirmation about how good you are. You can also use affirmations as a reminder for what you want to improve. Let's say you've noticed that you are struggling with being patient. Your affirmation may be "I deserve to take my time and enjoy doing the things I love." Another opportunity for positive self-talk is when you practice mindfulness. After you've focused on yourself by being mindful, say something that will encourage you and make you smile.

TRY THIS! MIRROR, MIRROR

Look at your reflection in a mirror and tell yourself five things you love about yourself. This can be anything, from your eyes to how caring you are toward a sibling or friend.

Write your list of things here. If you ever need a reminder, you can always pick up this book and find five positive things about yourself.

1. --

2. --

3. --

4. --

5. --

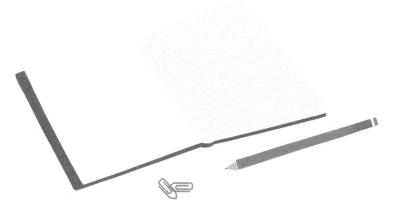

A way to practice positive self-talk is through **affirmations**. These are positive thoughts that you repeat to yourself. When you have an unhelpful thought, respond with an affirmation about how good you are. You can also use affirmations as a reminder for what you want to improve. Let's say you've noticed that you are struggling with being patient. Your affirmation may be "I deserve to take my time and enjoy doing the things I love." Another opportunity for positive self-talk is when you practice mindfulness. After you've focused on yourself by being mindful, say something that will encourage you and make you smile.

TRY THIS! MIRROR, MIRROR

Look at your reflection in a mirror and tell yourself five things you love about yourself. This can be anything, from your eyes to how caring you are toward a sibling or friend.

Write your list of things here. If you ever need a reminder, you can always pick up this book and find five positive things about yourself.

1. _____

2. _____

3. _____

4. _____

5. _____

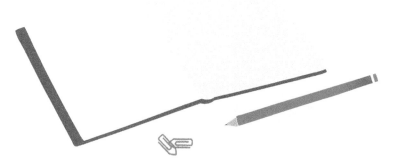

Unhelpful Thoughts

Unhelpful thoughts are when we think negative things. If you don't recognize unhelpful thoughts, they can become an automatic way of thinking. For example, imagine it is your first day at a new school and you're excited to make friends. You notice that most of the kids in your classes seem to have already made friends, so you keep telling yourself, "I'm not cool enough." When you repeat negative self-talk like this, it is called **rumination**. Over time, rumination can develop into a belief about yourself. This is called a **self-limiting belief**.

Rumination and self-limiting beliefs work together. When you ruminate, you change the way your brain naturally thinks. You place a limit on what you can or cannot do, and you develop a fixed mindset. Allowing unhelpful thoughts to ruminate and create self-limiting beliefs makes it very difficult to have a growth mindset. We all have unhelpful thoughts, but you have the power to change, ignore, or act on those thoughts.

Reframing Unhelpful Thoughts

Remember that reframing is when you notice unhelpful thoughts and transform them into useful, positive thoughts. When you ruminate on unhelpful thoughts, you begin to believe them to be true. This is why it helps to reframe. The way you think about what is happening affects the way you feel and behave.

Identifying unhelpful thoughts can sometimes be difficult. You may not even be aware of what is happening in your own mind, so it is important to check in on yourself. Whenever you feel sad, anxious, or uncomfortable, try to practice mindfulness. Notice any physical sensations. Are your palms sweaty? Are you tapping your foot or heels? Ask yourself questions like:

How else can I look at this situation?

Is this situation as bad as I am making it out to be?

What can I do to make things better?

Reframing your thoughts does not mean that you never have negative or unhelpful thoughts. It just means that you don't let those negative thoughts frame how you feel about yourself. By learning to recognize unhelpful thoughts and reframing them over time, you will shift to a growth mindset.

Picture yourself in the following scenario. Then use the script to ask yourself questions and practice how to reframe thoughts.

Scenario

You wake up late on Monday morning. In your rush to get to school, you leave your part of a group project at home. When you get to class and notice you don't have your work, you get angry. You start having negative thoughts about yourself, such as *I always let people down!*

Script

Am I jumping to negative conclusions?

How else can I look at this situation?

What's the worst and best things that can happen?

What can I learn from this situation that can help me in the future?

Mindfulness Tool Kit

Here are some mindful ways to develop a growth mindset. Think of these activities as tools in your mindfulness tool kit.

* **Keep a thought record.** Practice mindful reflection by writing down some of the thoughts you have throughout the day. See if you can identify helpful thoughts and unhelpful thoughts. Come up with one or two explanations for why the thought is not helpful. What was the **trigger** or situation that caused any unhelpful thoughts? Let your answers guide you to reframe the thought.

* **Belly breathe.** Place a hand on your stomach and take a deep breath. Inhale slowly through your nose, allowing the air to fill your belly. Hold the breath in for a count of four. Release. Repeat until you start to feel calm.

* **Color.** Coloring can ease stress by bringing your focus to the present moment. Draw a simple picture or pattern and then color it in a mindful way. Think about each color you choose and notice how you apply it.

Remember to be patient with yourself. Some of these activities may not be easy on your first try. The tools in this kit will become easier to use over time. A growth mindset means not giving up. Keep trying and improving!

Reflect on everything you have learned about mindfulness in this chapter. Remember that it's all about focusing on the present moment. Your brain is powerful enough to engage in many thoughts and feelings, but it helps to focus on one thing. Think about how a computer may slow down when you have multiple programs open at once. For this focus game, track how long it takes you to complete the following tasks.

Task 1: Write the letters of the alphabet from A to Z.

Task 2: Write the numbers from 1 to 26.

Task 3: Write the first letter followed by the first number (A1) and then the next letter and next number (B2) until you've reached Z26.

How long did tasks 1 and 2 combined take?

How long did task 3 take?

I
ENJOY
TRYING
NEW THINGS

CHAPTER FOUR

BEING BRAVE

ravery means having the strength to face challenges. Being brave is doing something even though you may be scared and not letting that fear stop you. There are many different ways to be brave, and they can all help you develop a growth mindset. Any time you persevere and overcome fear is an act of bravery.

Fear is all around us. It is normal to be fearful of doing something, especially for the first time. Think about some of the most challenging things you've dealt with. It could be riding a bike for the first time, traveling to school on your own, or being away from home at camp. If you've done any of those things, then you have added to your growth mindset. Fear is a human emotion that is programmed into the nervous system and works like an instinct. Sometimes fear can be unhelpful if it is irrational. An irrational fear is when something scares you but does not actually pose a danger to you. For example, your first time performing in a play may seem terrifying. But are you actually in danger? Being in front of an audience will not hurt you, so do not let fear take over.

Stepping Out of Your Comfort Zone

We all have activities and places in which we feel confident and comfortable. A lot of these things are tricky or feel unnatural at first. Then we become so good at them that they are no longer challenging or scary! Have you ever tried to play a new video game for the first time? Your hands probably struggled to figure out which buttons to press. It may have taken you hours to progress through a level. If you gave up and went back to an old game you've played many times before, that is an example of staying in your **comfort zone**. Comfort zones can be good for a place of safety. But if you stay in that place of ease for too long, you risk missing opportunities. The new video game could have given you hours of fun and the chance to bond with friends. Pushing yourself out of your comfort zone will give you a feeling of accomplishment.

It's Okay to Be Unsure

Our fears often come from the unknown. Meeting new people or trying new things can be scary. It's okay to feel unsure! You can embrace fear and use it to step outside your comfort zone.

Try these tips whenever you're feeling uncertain or scared.

* **Acknowledge your feelings.** Whether it is fear, anxiousness, or just uncertainty, telling yourself not to feel these emotions is unfair to you. You're feeling this way for a reason. Accept your feeling by saying, "I'm nervous because this is my first time doing this and I don't know what to expect."

* **Ask for help.** Speak to someone who has done what you are nervous about doing. Tell them your worries. Familiarity can often ease fears. If possible, have a trusted person walk you through the process.

* **Take small steps.** Becoming brave does not have to happen in an instant. Taking things slowly and seeing positive changes over time will gradually boost your confidence.

* **Visualize yourself succeeding.** If you're nervous about a race, try this mindfulness practice. Before the race, picture yourself running across the finish line and being surrounded by your loved ones.

* **See failure as a lesson.** Failure is less scary when you know you'll always learn how to be better through it.

Think of something new you want to learn or experience. Some examples include joining a club, having a difficult conversation, or learning a new language. Now map out a plan for it on the following page. In the first box, draw yourself doing something you are familiar with. In the second box, draw yourself trying your new thing. In the last box, draw yourself accomplishing this new thing. Use this map as a way to visualize your growth.

I CAN DO THIS!

COMFORT ZONE

LEARNING ZONE

GROWTH ZONE

Being Curious

Curiosity is the desire to know something through questions or observation. It is the driving force behind motivation. Being curious fuels your brain to remember the things you are learning. Without curiosity, we are more inclined to stay in a fixed mindset. You can embrace your curiosity and use it as motivation to face your fears. Curiosity is not limited to humans. All species who learn and grow do so through curiosity. Think about dogs. If they are curious about something, they look alert, and their ears and tail will be upright. When you take a dog for a walk, you'll notice that they will head directly toward something and often walk in circles around it, intently sniffing. That is curiosity. They want to know what they're smelling.

Here are some tips to help grow your curiosity:

* **Embrace your uncertainty.** Be grateful that you don't know everything and use that to learn new things.

* **Seek out information.** When something new catches your attention, challenge yourself to be curious and learn more about it.

* **Read something new every week.** It can be anything and doesn't have to take more than a few minutes.

Let's embrace curiosity by bonding with the people in your life. Your relatives and friends all have different areas of interest. You can learn things you would not have otherwise learned about them by being curious.

Pretend you're the host of a talk show. You can even give your show its own name. Invite someone you know to be a guest and ask them interview questions. Where were they born? Do they speak another language? What is a fun fact they would like to share? Tell them what you've learned so far in this book, and see if they have any stories of overcoming challenges.

Follow Your Ambitions

Ambition is the drive that makes you want to achieve something. Your ambitions can be anything you dream of doing, like learning to play guitar so you can start your own band. To achieve your ambition, you have to strive for it through desire and determination. So far in this chapter, you learned about overcoming fear, being brave, and stepping outside your comfort zone. Healthy ambition pushes you to successfully face challenges.

Sometimes having a lot of ambition can lead you to putting a lot of pressure on yourself. When this happens, be careful not to fall into unhelpful thoughts. Use all the tools you've learned so far to approach ambition in a healthy way. For example, reframe unhelpful thoughts so they don't block or limit your ambition. Use affirmations to remind you that you have the power to achieve your ambition. Remember that making mistakes is great for learning. Each and every setback makes you stronger and more equipped to deal with future setbacks. Chasing ambition can be tough. Be sure to use your growth mindset skills and find the joy in the journey.

Take a minute to think about three things you enjoy doing regularly. Maybe it's cooking, dancing, and playing hockey. Write these down in the first column. Now think about everything you have learned about ambition. In the second column, write a way you could approach this activity with ambition. Let this motivate you next time you do those things. One example has been shown for you.

THINGS I LOVE	AMBITIONS
Cooking	Prepare a meal for my entire family

GROWTH MINDSET IN ACTION

American inventor **THOMAS EDISON** once said, "You must learn to fail intelligently. Failing is one of the greatest arts in the world. One fails forward toward success." Edison was said to have failed thousands of times before finally making the first commercially successful light bulb in 1879. When he was working on a novel storage battery, he tried 9,000 experiments before he was able to find a solution. Over the course of his life, Thomas Edison invented more than 1,000 things, including the phonograph and motion picture. Thomas Edison showed perseverance by pushing through failures and using a growth mindset to reframe his mistakes.

Taking Healthy Risks

Part of having a growth mindset is taking risks. That means doing something that has the potential to end in a loss or failure. Some risks are dangerous and should never be tried. The type of risks we want to focus on are known as healthy risks. These are safe and help you learn and grow. Healthy risks include things like auditioning for a talent show, trying new hobbies, and running for class president.

Risks don't have to be scary. Here is a strategy for figuring out if a risk is worth taking. Just ask yourself these questions:

* What will I gain from taking this risk?

* What would anyone else gain from taking this risk?

* Would an adult be proud of me for doing this?

* What lessons can I learn from doing this?

Keep the benefits of healthy risk-taking in mind. Some benefits include increasing your self-esteem and taking on more responsibilities in your life.

Taking risks can be scary! But don't let that fear or uncertainty stop you from learning something new. Consider the following before you take a risk and while taking the risk:

Practice positive self-talk. This will improve your self-esteem and encourage you as you try to overcome any fears you may have.

Persist. Push through and complete the task even when things get difficult.

Ask for help if you need it. Taking on a healthy risk does not mean you have to do it alone.

Be kind to yourself. Stop or take a break when your mind or body is struggling or exhausted.

Push past your comfort zone. Know where this zone ends and your growth zone begins. Go further, and don't be afraid of making mistakes.

What If It Goes Wrong?

Taking risks means that there is a chance it may go "wrong." Sometimes we fear taking risks because we overthink. We focus too much on all the things that could go wrong. Imagine you have been excited to learn how to swim. In the days leading up to your swim class, you begin to worry. You start to tell yourself that you won't be able to float in the water. It just doesn't seem possible. The day before class, you start to have a stomachache.

What you have been going through is called a worry cycle. This is a pattern of negative thoughts that continues on and on. Worry cycles can block your growth mindset because they can stop you from trying new things.

If you find yourself in a worry cycle, remind yourself that it is okay to be afraid. In this case, acknowledge your fear of swimming. Then reframe the unhelpful thoughts and self-doubt: "I can learn. There will be an instructor there to help me. I will wear a life vest to protect me." This reframing will help push you through your comfort zone to an area where you can grow and learn.

Building Confidence

Confidence is the feeling or belief that you can do something. It's all about trusting yourself. Along with bravery, confidence is a powerful tool to have in your growth mindset tool kit. Being confident will allow you to take healthy risks without falling into a worry cycle. Everyone has different levels of confidence. Their level changes depending on what the challenge is. You may be very confident in your singing abilities, and your confidence shows by how quickly you learn new music. On the other hand, you may not be so confident in your athletic abilities. You may need quite a few drills before you get the hang of soccer. That can be frustrating, but it is totally normal! No one is perfect at anything on the first try. Your confidence will help you persevere in these instances.

There are a bunch of things you can do to improve your confidence. Here are a few to try:

* **Positive affirmations.** If you lack confidence in yourself, a daily reminder of how awesome you are can help.

* **Celebrate all your wins.** No matter how small it may be, every win is a step in the right direction. Pat yourself on the back anytime you complete a task or make someone smile, for example.

* **Be kind to yourself.** No one person has all the confidence in the world. Confidence is often built over time and through experiences. Being kind builds self-esteem, which will allow your confidence to grow.

Imagine you have a piano recital or an important tennis match—something for which you've been practicing for months. You've always felt that you would do well. As you get dressed, you start feeling nervous and unsure.

Draw a comic that shows this experience. Include speech bubbles of things you might say, like positive affirmations you would tell yourself. In the last comic panel, show yourself succeeding at the thing you've been practicing.

I SEE
FAILURES
AS OPPORTUNITIES
FOR GROWTH

CHAPTER FIVE

WE ALL MAKE MISTAKES

CHAPTER FIVE
WE ALL MAKE MISTAKES

Everyone makes mistakes, whether they're an expert at something or just a beginner. It may seem like it would be ideal to start something and finish it without any problems. But mistakes are an incredibly valuable tool to help you learn and grow.

Pobody's Nerfect

One of the biggest obstacles to a growth mindset is the desire to be perfect. But doing something perfectly is not possible because—say it with me—NOBODY IS PERFECT!

Perfectionism is when you strive so hard to be perfect that you refuse to accept anything less—from yourself or from anyone else. An example of this is when you won't perform with the dance team because the team members aren't performing the choreography exactly in sync. Such perfectionism hurts you because you no longer experience the joy of performing and your teammates were counting on you.

Unrealistic expectations will only make you super frustrated when you or those around you fail to live up to them. When this happens, you might give up all together. People who are overly critical may blame themselves in every negative situation. They get down on themselves as a person rather than the specific mistakes they make. They often avoid taking healthy risks.

If someone is a perfectionist, they might struggle to build a growth mindset. Trying to be perfect can keep you from enjoying activities and starting new hobbies. This is because you'll be worried about not making any mistakes. Try the following to help you overcome perfectionism.

Self-compassion. Compassion is recognizing when other people are struggling and taking action to care for them. At times, it can be easier to be compassionate toward others rather than yourself. When you're struggling with a tough task, tell yourself that this is a learning process and you're doing your best.

Balance self-improvement with self-acceptance. Never tell yourself that you are not good enough. Instead, remind yourself that there is room for improvement! Accept your areas of growth while working to improve them.

Remember to have fun. Make it a point to enjoy what you are doing. If you notice a lack of joy, take a little break and do something that makes you happy.

Write down what "perfect" means to you in this moment.

Now let's explore this definition. What happens when you understand that perfection is only an idea? Even cooler, what happens when the definition is up to you? In this exercise, you can change the word "perfect" to mean whatever you want. If "perfect" means to you that you just made a fun mistake because you tried something new, then that's what it means! In this way, "perfect" is what you want it to be, not what someone else wants it to be for you.

List three or four activities and come up with new definitions of "perfect" for those activities. If you write down "playing guitar," maybe the new definition of perfect is "playing a new song with lots of mistakes." Don't be afraid to dream up something wild! This is your vision of perfection.

ACTIVITY	NEW "PERFECT"

New Goal

Rather than reaching for perfection, aim to make a real effort and keep working. Everyone who is great at something started out this way! Set goals that don't require you to be perfect. Let's say you have a goal to journal every day. Start by setting a goal to write in your journal three times a week. This can help you build the habit and get you closer to your overall goal. If your larger goal is to join the chess team, you can start by giving yourself a time to practice daily. Knowing you don't have to be the best chess player before you join will take out a lot of the stress. You can just focus on improving as preparation for the team tryout. If you struggle with waking up on time for school every day, set a goal to wake up on time twice next week.

Make Mistakes Your Friends

The key to having a growth mindset is understanding that mistakes happen to everyone. In fact, mistakes are good! It is the *fear* of making mistakes that blocks you. People with growth mindsets are very eager to make a second or third go while incorporating all the lessons they've learned from prior mistakes. This perseverance often leads to great things.

Oops!

You may feel a variety of emotions after making a mistake. These may include frustration, sadness, anger, or defeat. Do you recall ever feeling these ways? If so, you are in the majority. Most people feel one of these ways after making mistakes. Each of these feelings is valid. You may feel like the mistake could have been avoided, but don't let this slow you down from reaching your goal. Try the following to help you move through difficult emotions that may come up when mistakes are made.

Name the emotion. Instead of saying, "I am afraid," say, "This is fear." Identifying the emotion allows you to acknowledge it while also empowering you to separate yourself from it. *You* are not afraid; you are *feeling* afraid.

Avoid dwelling. Spending too much time thinking about the mistake can make you feel even worse. Learn from it, and then give yourself permission to let it go. Then do something you enjoy!

Do something that can put you in a different mood. Sometimes doing the opposite of the difficult emotion can help you move past it. If you're feeling unsuccessful, pick up a puzzle or get out your pencils and draw. Do anything you are good at.

Think about a time you made a mistake in school or at home. While you're thinking about this mistake, pay close attention to how you feel in your body. Say the feeling that comes up, like disappointed, discouraged, mad, and so on. Take a slow, deep breath in through your nose while counting to three. Then exhale out through your mouth and count to three. Say the following statement:

> This mistake will help me
> learn and grow.

Repeat this a few times. This intentional breathing will help you reflect on your mistake and refocus it as an opportunity.

Learning from Mistakes

Whether it's a sport, a musical instrument, or a magic trick, learning something new involves making mistakes. Learning from mistakes is how we challenge ourselves to do things a different way. It forces us to innovate how we problem-solve. It helps us think outside the box to see things in different ways. Mistakes encourage us to be brave and take healthy risks. If you make a mistake, take the time to praise yourself for even trying in the first place. You cannot improve at something if you don't practice! Feeling good about trying will encourage you to learn from your mistakes and try again.

I'M PROUD OF MYSELF FOR TRYING.

Think of a mistake you have made, whether large or small. This could be that you missed an important deadline for a class project or you hurt a friend's feelings by not remembering their birthday. It can be something that happened today or even a few years ago. Take this opportunity to reflect on the mistake. Write out the lessons you learned and how you can use these lessons in the future.

My mistake was

A lesson I learned is

In the future, I will

Taking Responsibility

Your brain is still growing until you become an adult. Research has shown that young brains lack the full ability to make decisions on the same level that adults do. What does this mean? Basically, it's okay for you to make mistakes! What's important is to take responsibility for those mistakes. This will help you fix them as quickly and painlessly as possible. Don't ignore your mistakes or brush them aside. For example, say you go meet up with friends and remember that you left the bathroom sink running. The quicker you tell someone at home, the less likely it will cause any water damage or get you in bigger trouble.

It can be tough to own up to your mistakes, but like everything else, it gets easier the more you practice! Think about how you feel. Are you worried about how the other person may react? Don't let the feelings stop you from talking. Instead, allow your feelings to be part of the conversation. Put your feelings into words. You could say something like "I need to talk to you about what happened, but I am a little embarrassed." Practice how you'll start the conversation. Having a plan will help remove the fear of the unknown.

GROWTH MINDSET
IN ACTION

TYLER PERRY is an actor, director, producer, and writer. He had a very difficult upbringing as a middle child of four who grew up in poverty. His life started to shift after watching an episode of *The Oprah Winfrey Show*. The show told him that sometimes troubles can be worked through if you write them down. His first journal was filled with letters to himself, which led to the first play he wrote, *I Know I've Been Changed*. Tyler managed to save up some money and rented a theater to perform the play. After all his efforts, only thirty people showed up for the first weekend of performances. Tyler did not give up after this. For the next six years, he worked different jobs to keep the show in production. Sometimes he even lived on the street because he could not afford to pay rent. Finally, the show received the reception he was hoping for. Through his perseverance, he became a success and went on to a successful film career.

Celebrating Your Mistakes

By now, you know mistakes are common and that learning from mistakes is a part of how we challenge ourselves. It motivates us to do things differently, to be creative and flexible in our approach to life. That's why you should celebrate your mistakes. Really! Am I asking you to be happy and jump for joy when you make mistakes? Well, yes and no. You should not actively seek out mistakes to make. But catching a mistake and using it to improve yourself is worth celebrating.

When you make a mistake, think about what you've learned from it and acknowledge how far you've already come. For example, if you're working on a science experiment and it's still not going your way after a few attempts, use the power of "yet" to celebrate: "I can't find the solution to this experiment . . . *yet*." Keep track of your mistakes in a "FAIL" (First Attempt in Learning) journal. Go back and check off your challenges once you've succeeded. You might even be able to use one of those failed ideas successfully for another project! Another way to celebrate? Tell your friends and family all about what happened and what you learned from the experience. Reframe that mistake into a positive.

⚡ TRY THIS! ACCIDENTAL MASTERPIECE ⚡

Grab some crayons, markers, or colored pencils. Pick the colors you use the least. Place all of the coloring tools in a bag. Shake the bag so the colors are all mixed up and randomly grab a tool from the bag without looking. Whatever color you take out, you must use it somewhere on the following illustration. Continue until you have completed coloring the page. You'll notice that you've used uncommon colors for certain objects. Take a look at your masterpiece and be proud of your creativity. Some might see a red lake as a mistake, but you turned it into art.

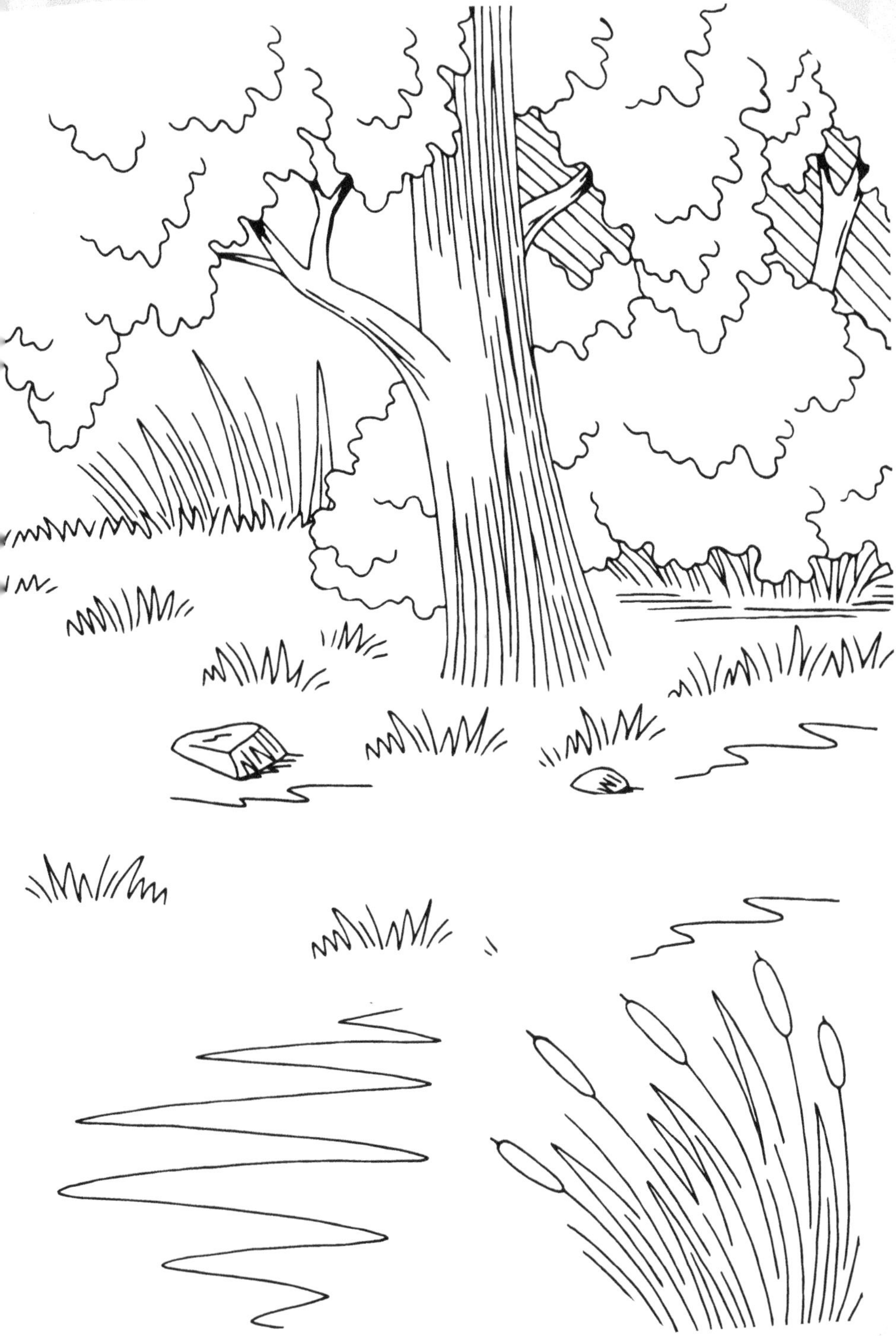

Try Again!

At the beginning of this book, we explored perseverance in the face of obstacles. Remember that it's important to be **resilient** and keep trying. Don't give up! How else can you measure improvements and learn from mistakes if you are not trying again and again? Lessons are valuable. Some lessons can only be learned from trying to do something. Improving your growth mindset involves a willingness to apply the lessons learned from mistakes.

Practice Makes Perfect

Practice is how we make progress. Just like you are using this book to practice the skills to develop a growth mindset, you can practice in lots of different ways to help you grow in other areas. It takes time and patience to practice anything. Be intentional on what you are focusing your energy on. Intentional practice means finding out what you know and what you need to improve. You can ask a friend, teacher, or coach to help guide you with feedback. If you're practicing something you already know, you won't see as much growth, and it can be harder to commit. Just keep trying until you're confident you've given your best. Progress requires you to keep working on your areas of growth until you've mastered them. Don't cheat yourself out of your growth by not practicing effectively.

The Power of "Yet"

Words have power. "I can't complete this puzzle" is different from "I can't complete this puzzle *yet*." Do you see how "yet" is such a powerful and affirming word? Adding "yet" to the end of a thought transforms your perspective. This helps you become more open to learning from mistakes. When you say this word, you're saying that if you can't do something now, you will eventually. The best way to start using the power of "yet" is to be aware of all the times you use the word "can't." Once you notice the word "can't," add "yet" to the end.

I can't do a handstand . . . **YET.**

I can't sing this harmony . . . **YET.**

I can't solve this math problem . . . **YET.**

You've just successfully reframed your unhelpful thought into a positive thought!

TRY THIS! SUCCESS PLANNING

Now it is time for you to apply the power of "yet." Create a list of things you'd like to do that you are unable to do now. Then give yourself a time for when you will be able to do each thing. Really push yourself to think of things that you can do with some guidance and practice.

THING I CAN'T DO YET	HOW AND WHEN I'LL BE ABLE TO DO IT
1. _____ _____ _____ _____	1. _____ _____ _____ _____
2. _____ _____ _____ _____	2. _____ _____ _____ _____
3. _____ _____ _____ _____	3. _____ _____ _____ _____

Feedback Helps You Learn

You are surrounded by people who want to see you succeed in everything you do. Listening to their feedback is part of how you will become the best person you can be. Being able to receive constructive feedback is a growth mindset skill. It is important because there are tons of things you just are not able to do yet. On the journey of trying things out and practicing, you will need help from people along the way. Not all types of feedback are necessarily helpful. This includes words that sound and feel like personal attacks, which have very little to do with the task at hand. If you are unsure whether a piece of feedback is constructive, take some time to think and reflect on it. Perhaps share it with someone you trust. The intent behind feedback is important. Constructive criticism should be honest and helpful, not hurtful. It should assist you by pointing out areas you can focus on for improvement.

Here are some examples of constructive and nonconstructive feedback:

Nonconstructive: I can't believe you missed the soccer goal.

Constructive: Great try! Let's work together as a team on your shooting technique.

Nonconstructive: You created such a mess in the kitchen when you made breakfast. You should know better.

Constructive: The pancakes you made were delicious. Nice job! If you rinse the batter from the mixing bowl before it dries, it will be much easier to clean. Then you can go out and have fun more quickly!

WHEN I'M
FRUSTRATED
I KEEP
TRYING

CHAPTER SIX
READY FOR THE NEXT CHALLENGE

Facing new challenges isn't always easy. It can bring up frustration, and we might feel resistant. Resistance is refusing to accept something, especially when it's tough to deal with. The key is to pay attention to those emotions and listen to them. Then you can figure out what they're trying to tell you.

Frustration Is Expected

Challenges are an expected part of life—you are not alone in having to face them! Unfortunately, knowing that challenges are coming doesn't always ease the stress that comes with them. When you meet obstacles, it is normal to feel frustration. This is your body telling you that you're in unfamiliar territory. You may feel the same way when you're struggling with a difficult homework assignment, for example. There are a few different ways to cope with frustrations and reframe them.

* **Ask for help.** It is okay to seek help to overcome challenges. Asking for assistance does not make you weak.

* **Practice mindfulness.** Mindfulness is a powerful tool when it comes to dealing with frustration. Find a quiet space if you can and focus on your breathing. Breathe in deeply and then hold it in for five seconds. Gently release it for five seconds. Repeat this five times to help calm you.

* **Redirect your emotions.** Some people can do a quick breathing exercise and be ready to work. Others may need more time. Take a break from what you're doing. You could go for a walk, get some water, or just do something that makes you feel great. When you're ready, come back and try again.

Answer the questions to identify how your body responds when you are frustrated. Then use this thermometer to gauge your levels of frustration. Look at the coping skills on the right. Draw a line from each skill to the part of the thermometer that designates when it might most help you release stress.

What is a sign that you are not frustrated?

What is a sign that you are very frustrated?

What is a sign that you are mildly frustrated?

----

very
frustrated

mildly
frustrated

no
frustration

Take a time-out

Take a walk

Do yoga

Read a book

Play some music

Play a game

Talk to someone

Embracing Challenges

There are many different responses you can have to frustration. Some shut down and become quiet. Others cry because they feel angry or sad. Those feelings may be so overwhelming that they seem like the end of the world—but they are not.

Turn Frustration into Action

Try turning frustration and limiting beliefs into helpful actions by taking the following steps.

1. **Identify the real reason you are frustrated.** What was the trigger? This context will help you figure out which action you can take to ease the frustration.

2. **Get some fresh air when possible.** Going outside can do your body good. While you're doing so, be mindful. Pause to notice your surroundings and breathe deeply.

3. **Make a plan.** Having a plan can bring a sense of calmness and peace. Your plan can be as simple as breaking down the task into smaller steps. Spread the steps out over a period of time or just establish which order to do each step.

4. **Look for solutions, not problems.** Create a list of possible solutions. This helps you remember that the problem is fixable.

There are many ways to work through frustration. Let's see if you can identify the healthy ways to respond to yours.

1. What should you do when you notice you are becoming frustrated?
   a. Ignore the feeling.
   b. Pause, take a deep breath, and identify what is causing the frustration.

2. To practice mindfulness, you should focus your attention on which of the following?
   a. The task that is frustrating you.
   b. The inhale and exhale of your breath.

3. Looking for solutions to the problem is a useful way to deal with frustration because it reminds you that the problem can be fixed.
   a. True
   b. False

4. Making a plan in response to frustration can help bring a sense of calm.

   a. True

   b. False

5. How do you redirect your attention?

   a. Focus on a different part of the problem.

   b. Focus your attention on something totally different, like taking a walk.

Answers: 1: b; 2: b; 3: a; 4: a; 5: b

Focus on What You Can Control

Dwelling on the things you can't control often distracts from what you *can* control. Focusing on things in your control will often increase your self-esteem. If you've ever played a sport, you may have already experienced this. You can practice and be the very best in your position, but if a teammate makes a mistake or if the opposing team works better as a group, your team might lose. Is that your fault? No. Will you still feel disappointed about the result? Sure! But you can't control what others do or don't do. Instead, focus on what *you* can do—and do it to the best of your ability. This will help you move forward when you're faced with a difficult challenge.

Reframing can be a helpful tool to turn negative thoughts into opportunities for change and growth. It also helps you transform your point of view. Use this script to guide yourself back to the things you can control. Answering these questions will take the blame off yourself for failures that are out of your control.

Is worrying about this going to change the outcome in any way?

What are some other possible reasons this could have happened? Was any of this in my control?

What more could I have done?

Remember That Change Is Good!

Do you ever get bored? It happens when your mind is not being stimulated or when you are not enjoying the task or experience at hand. This is why change is good. Imagine being in the school band and your only task is to strike the drum after each person's solo. How long do you think you'd enjoy doing this before it becomes boring? You most likely wouldn't want to join the band the next school year unless you were given new responsibilities. When everything remains the same, you're no longer excited or pushing yourself to your full potential. Change happens all around us—it's inevitable! Next school year, you will face new challenges in the form of new classmates, new teachers, maybe even an entirely new school. That's how you continue to grow and learn!

GROWTH MINDSET
IN ACTION

ABRAHAM LINCOLN was a successful self-taught lawyer before he became president of the United States. In 1855, he was hired to work on a case that he immediately recognized as an opportunity to move his career forward. He deep-dived into trial preparation, learning everything he could about the technology that was central to the case. When the trial moved to another state, he was removed from the case—but no one told him! He showed up ready to work, but when he was told he wasn't needed, Abraham didn't angrily pack his bags and head home. He stayed for the entire trial. Abraham wasn't a trained lawyer, but these men were, and he studied them carefully. He took notes on how they crafted their arguments and spoke to witnesses. He recognized these men were far better lawyers than himself. He vowed in that moment to go home, study law, and push himself to become a better lawyer. Instead of crumbling in the face of a setback, Abraham used it as inspiration to grow his abilities and ambitions.

Healthy Competition

Being competitive is normal. In fact, people can be competitive when they are not even aware of it. Healthy competition can motivate us to do great things. It helps us develop **empathy**, resilience, and perseverance. But unhealthy competition may bring on too much unnecessary pressure. It can lead to negative self-talk and damage self-esteem.

Healthy competition is not about the outcome, and it's not about winning. Instead, it's about enjoyment and learning things along the way. Beating your personal best time in a race or successfully using a new technique in a game are examples of healthy competition.

On the other hand, unhealthy competition creates feelings of frustration if things don't go your way. Say you enter a competition with a friend to see who can finish a puzzle the quickest. You work extremely hard, but your friend finishes before you. You become angry with yourself. You've let what started as a friendly competition turn into something unhealthy. How do you engage in competition without feeling frustrated or angry? Have fun and focus on what you can control. You cannot control how fast your friend completes the puzzle. So put your energy into enjoying the process, trying your best, and remembering that you can always get better.

Play a game of freeze tag with your friends. You'll need at least four people. The object of the game is to avoid being tagged. Pick a player who is "it"—they have to chase the other players and tag them by tapping them lightly. When you are tagged, you must remain still for ten seconds. After that time, you are free to move around and unfreeze any other players by tapping them. Unlike other games of tag, there is no winner. After five minutes, the game is over. Instead of playing to win, simply enjoy the game and not the result.

Handling Rejection

Everyone gets rejected at some point, and it will happen many times throughout your life. You won't make every team you try out for, you won't get invited to some sleepovers, and you won't always land the lead role in the school play. The trick is not allowing rejection to impact your self-esteem. You're *still* awesome!

At first, you might try to dismiss or downplay the rejection. But this can make you feel isolated. Instead, name your feelings and reflect on the rejection. You must acknowledge what happened before you can work through it. You can also tell someone how you feel. Sometimes it can be reassuring to know that others may feel the same way you feel.

Whatever you do, try not to dwell on it. When you're dealing with rejection, it's easy to get stuck in unhelpful thought patterns. But this only makes you relive the painful rejection. Allow yourself to safely do something that makes you feel better.

Let's practice healthy ways to handle rejection. All you need is a pencil or pen to use as a spinner. Now imagine you told a joke to a group of people and nobody laughed. This is an everyday situation that can cause feelings of rejection.

1. Lay the pen or pencil over the game board and spin it.

2. Whatever piece you land on, practice this response to the rejection.

Be honest about your feelings of rejection.

Give yourself credit for trying.

Don't rush yourself to get over the feeling.

Do something nice for yourself.

Appreciate all the other good things going for you.

Talk to someone who may understand.

I ASK
FOR HELP
WHEN
I NEED IT

CHAPTER SEVEN
WE'RE ALL IN THIS TOGETHER

Everyone will encounter challenges throughout their lives. Challenges can bring up a lot of emotions, and these emotional responses can be different for everyone. Always remember that you are not alone. When you're going through a tough time, seek support from friends, trusted adults, and resources in your community.

Talk It Out

Society sometimes tells boys they shouldn't cry, ask for help, or even talk about their emotions. It often seems like it is only acceptable for girls to do these things. This is completely false. People of all genders have a wide range of emotions. The same thing that upsets your sister or friend can be upsetting to you as well. Sharing your emotions with a person you trust is a helpful strategy. Often, that person may be able to relate to you and offer advice that helped them in the past.

When you talk it out, you are less likely to get depressed. You never want to hold on to negative feelings and thoughts for too long. If you do, they can intensify and have lasting effects on your mood and personality. Speaking about these feelings can be a useful way to unburden yourself and will make you feel so much better.

Practice being **vulnerable**. Vulnerability allows you the opportunity to connect with others who may have similar experiences as you. Hearing "I feel the same way" can be a big push to try again. These words also remind you that you are not alone.

Asking for Help

The most difficult part about asking for help can be knowing whom you can trust. You want to know who will be there for you without judgment. Once you've identified those people, asking for help becomes easier to do. You start allowing your trusted people to help you when needed. These people don't have to be adults, although they can be. Depending on the situation, you may feel more comfortable sharing your feelings with a sibling or a friend who will listen with compassion and understanding. You might also find trust with teachers, neighbors, or coaches. When we talk about our challenges with others, we often discover that they have encountered similar problems. They may have solutions we hadn't even considered!

Start a conversation! Identify one or two trusted adults in your life and talk with them. Ask them about times they've made mistakes and overcome challenges. Remember to ask very detailed questions and listen carefully. Here are a few examples to get you started.

1. What was the mistake?

2. How did you feel in the moment?

3. What steps did you take to overcome your challenges?

4. If you could do it over, what would you do differently?

GROWTH MINDSET
IN ACTION

KAUÃ RODOLFO was eleven years old when he became an ambassador for Plant-for-the-Planet, an environmental awareness organization led by kids. At a young age, he witnessed landslides, oil spills, and forest fires in his home in Brazil. Having lived through these natural disasters would be enough to scare anyone. But Kauã pushed through that fear and decided that it was his responsibility to help. He started planting trees in the Brazilian city of Curitiba to help save the environment. "I'm not scared of the future of the planet, because I'm going to help the planet," he said. "I'm going to do this. I'm going to go forward with this project. You don't have to be scared." Kauã persevered despite his fear and found courage in his convictions.

Communication 101

Communication is an important part of having a growth mind-set. To be most effective in communicating with others, try some of the following approaches.

Ask questions. Curious about something? Speak up! Don't be afraid to raise your hand in class or ask someone about a topic that interests them. You might discover a new favorite hobby or different way of doing things.

Seek out support. Can't quite reach your goal of selling forty candy boxes for that team fundraiser? Ask for help from your family members or anyone in your support network to achieve your goals. It's okay to reach out to more than one person if you need more help.

Share your feelings. Sometimes having too much on your mind can be distracting. Try speaking up about how you're feeling. This can make room for new helpful information.

Find information. Use all of your resources: textbooks, notes, videos, whatever you have access to. Preparing yourself for the task at hand will help you communicate more clearly.

Show gratitude. Be thankful to anyone and everyone who helps you achieve a goal. Not only will this make you feel good, but they'll be even happier to help you in the future if you say thanks!

Having conversations with adults can be weird and awkward sometimes. This can be because you're shy or because some topics make you anxious. You might just be nervous about how the conversation might go. Believe it or not, adults have some of these same concerns as well!

Try starting your conversation like this:

> Hi, I want to talk to you about _____.
> When do you think would be a good time?

From there, be mindful to be respectful; use full, clear sentences; always make good eye contact; and end by saying:

> Thank you for taking time to talk to me about this.

Whether the conversation goes the way you anticipated or not, always practice gratitude.

Listen Like a Pro

Listening to others is an important part of developing a growth mindset. To help you become a good listener, try some of the following strategies.

Focus your attention. Make good eye contact by looking at the other person's eyes when they talk. Turn toward them to clearly communicate your interest.

Listen to understand, not to respond. Imagine you are having a bad day and you try to talk to a friend about it. Instead of listening to you, they keep cutting you off and saying things they think you want to hear. How would this feel? Sometimes you just want someone to hear you and show empathy, not try to fix anything.

Confirm your understanding. Ask questions to clarify what you have heard or try repeating what you think the other person said. Did you fully understand what they said and how they said it? Checking will show that you care about what they're saying.

Pay attention to nonverbal cues. Nonverbal cues are the ways we look, move, and react when we communicate. Listening like a pro is paying attention to what someone is saying with their face and body. Your body language and your facial expressions can often say more than words.

TRY THIS! STORY CHAIN

Try listening like a pro with this story game. Find two or more people to play with you. To begin, one person starts an original story by saying one line. For example, "Once upon a time, there was a boy who had to present a history report in class." Then take turns, with each person repeating the lines that came before and adding one line to the story. Go around the circle two or three times more so everyone can add a couple lines. Were you able to repeat everything correctly?

Be Your Own Best Friend

You should always be compassionate toward others, but showing yourself compassion is important, too! Self-compassion is the ability to be understanding, accepting, and loving to yourself, especially during difficult times. For most people, it is easier to extend compassion to others than it is to provide for themselves. But we should all treat ourselves kindly! It will make us happier, more confident, and more motivated to tackle those tough challenges. As you try new things and make mistakes, practice self-compassion as you learn and grow. Remember, nothing is easy the first time. You might continue struggling on the second or third time or even more! You may become frustrated and have unhelpful thoughts, but that's normal. When you get discouraged, try practicing self-care. Think of some activities that you enjoy doing. On days you don't feel your best, do one of those activities to uplift your mood.

Another way to show yourself compassion is by talking to yourself the way you would to your best friend. Would you say something negative or discouraging when they are struggling? Of course not! You would support and encourage them. Do the same for yourself. Spending time with people who make you feel good will also help. Avoid those who make you doubt yourself and your abilities.

TRY THIS! SELF-CARE FINDER

Self-care helps relax our minds and bodies. Find nine examples of self-care in the following word search. Then check off the activities that you will try the next time you need to treat yourself with compassion.

```
C  I  J  S  J  U  R  C  M  C
Z  X  G  O  C  H  W  Z  U  N
O  M  D  I  U  H  Q  G  H  S
R  E  R  R  O  R  Y  O  G  A
E  D  A  E  B  M  N  U  C  G
S  I  W  A  H  A  K  A  J  S
T  T  W  D  B  E  T  V  L  I
T  A  A  O  D  U  S  H  D  N
G  T  L  O  B  S  G  Z  S  G
J  E  K  I  C  V  P  Y  Y  C
```

☐ bath   ☐ meditate   ☐ sing

☐ draw   ☐ read   ☐ walk

☐ journal   ☐ rest   ☐ yoga

Showing Empathy

The compassion we show ourselves should also be extended to others who are dealing with their own frustrations, setbacks, and mistakes. This is called empathy. When a friend is frustrated and you feel sad for them, providing soothing and hopeful words is a way to show empathy. Even though you are not directly experiencing their frustration, you are able to understand how they feel. Here are some strategies for showing empathy to others.

* **Put yourself in the other person's shoes.** Ask yourself, "How would I feel if it were me in this situation? How would I want to be treated?"

* **Recognize your shared experience.** Is this something that you have felt before? Let the other person know they are not alone. You have also felt that way in the past.

* **Don't try to fix anything.** Often, what a friend needs most is for you to simply be present and listen.

* **Don't make assumptions.** No assumption you make will ever fully fit how the person is feeling. This makes it difficult to establish an honest connection with the person.

Developing empathy is a skill that will need lots of practice. The more you do, the better you'll be able to show empathy to others.

Put yourself in someone else's shoes with this empathy game. All you need is a die. If you don't have a die, you can write the numbers 1 to 6 on small slips of paper and put them in a hat.

Roll the die or pick a number from the hat. Whatever number you get, imagine yourself in the matching situation. What are you feeling? How would you want someone to support you?

1. A friend's pet ran away.

2. A cousin did not make the soccer team.

3. A friend was not invited to a party, but you were.

4. A classmate failed a test.

5. A classmate left their lunch at home.

6. It rained today, and your sibling forgot their umbrella and got drenched.

I WILL
CELEBRATE
MY
SUCCESSES

CHAPTER EIGHT
LIMITLESS POTENTIAL

Your potential is limitless. That means there is nothing you cannot do if you continue building your growth mindset. Do not let obstacles and mistakes derail you. These things will happen throughout your entire life. You have so many resources to help guide you, starting with this book.

Let Yourself Shine!

You are special. There is no one else on Earth like you. Being authentic means recognizing and acknowledging your feelings, whether they are positive or negative, and acting in ways that match your values. To be authentic is to be brave! We all have parts of ourselves that we want or need to improve. Maybe you need to work on your patience. Maybe you're still working on your ability to limit distractions so you become better at completing goals. No matter what you're working on, remember what you've learned about self-compassion and empathy. Self-compassion is treating yourself kindly by being warm and understanding when things don't go your way. Empathy helps you understand how others are feeling. Practicing both will help you be your authentic self.

That Grass Looks Greener

A huge part of letting yourself shine is knowing your strengths and your areas of growth. Everyone has strengths, weaknesses, successes, and failures. No one is better than anyone else, including you! Comparing yourself to others is natural. We all do it sometimes. But it can cause high levels of anxiety and stress, so try to avoid doing it. Let's take a look at some ways you can avoid the comparison trap.

Every time you compare yourself to others, acknowledge it. Say something like "I just did it again. I compared myself to . . ." Comparing yourself can become an automatic response when you fall short of a goal. Instead of comparing yourself to another person, acknowledge that you fell short. Then think about what you could have done differently.

Strengthen your own sense of self-worth. As you are growing up and figuring out your identity and passions, remember that you are one of a kind. Your thoughts and feelings are yours and only yours. Know how special you are and continue improving yourself.

Turn the comparison into gratitude. Challenge yourself to find something to be thankful for. For example, "I am thankful that I had the opportunity to play in the tennis tournament, even though I did not win."

TRY THIS! DRAW A SELFIE

A self-portrait is a way to reflect on the unique qualities that make you who you are without comparing yourself to anyone else. In the space that follows, draw what represents your inner strength and the special powers you possess. You can include symbols, shapes, or friends and family members who support you. For a bonus challenge, try to do this without using any written words.

GROWTH MINDSET IN ACTION

CESAR CHAVEZ was a cofounder of the United Farm Workers of America, the first farm labor union in the United States. He was a strong advocate for migrant workers (those who move from place to place to find work). His advocacy drew national attention to appalling working conditions, resulting in reforms. Cesar defended the rights of farmworkers by organizing nonviolent protests, marches, and boycotts to fight for fair labor contracts with higher wages and improved working conditions. To create his union, he had to overcome huge opposition from California's agricultural businesses. He channeled his feelings of frustration over his own childhood of picking grapes and cotton in terrible conditions. Cesar used his empathy for the migrant workers to propel him forward and work hard even when it felt like everyone was against him. His slogan, "*Sí se puede*" ("Yes we can")—which President Obama adopted for his own campaign—exemplified Cesar's grit and determination.

Making Your Dreams Come True

We all have dreams—not the ones that happen at night when we sleep. These dreams are the things, big and small, that we want to achieve in life. It could be a job we want to have one day or giving a speech as the valedictorian at graduation. No one can achieve their biggest dreams without overcoming setbacks and obstacles along the journey. Don't worry, though! There are a variety of strategies you can use to overcome these challenges and achieve your dreams.

Setting Goals

There are two types of goals: long-term goals and short-term goals. Long-term goals are things you want to achieve months or years down the line, like being the starter on your school basketball team next season. Short-term goals are things you want to accomplish sooner rather than later, like trying to beat a video game in one weekend. To achieve long-term goals, it helps to break them down into a series of more achievable short-term goals.

Ask yourself these five questions anytime you set a goal.

1. What do I want to achieve? Be specific about what you want.

2. How will I track the progress of this goal?

3. Is this goal something that I can achieve? Keep it realistic.

4. Does this goal match my values and interests?

5. When will I achieve this goal? Set a timeline.

For example, let's say you want to start a science club. You can be specific by saying the club will have ten members and membership lasts for three months. The members will plan to meet twice a week from 3:15 to 4:15 in the afternoon. By the end of three months, the club will present a project on sedimentary rocks. This is a great goal because it answers the five preceding questions.

TRY THIS! GOAL SETTING

Now that you know what makes a successful goal, see if you can identify some. Remember the five things you need to make a goal: be specific, make it trackable, make it achievable, make it relevant, and set a date to achieve the goal. Are these goals successful?

Yes   No

☐   ☐   1.   I want to develop a morning routine so I won't be late for school.

☐   ☐   2.   I will meet with each of my teachers within the first two weeks of classes to build a relationship with them and understand their expectations.

☐   ☐   3.   This year, I will complete all my assignments at least one day before they are due to avoid rushing and messing up. To do this, I will list all of my assignments in order of their due dates and work on them in that order. I will spend fifteen minutes every Sunday night identifying which assignments need my attention during the week.

☐   ☐   4.   I'm going to start doing all my chores in one day so I won't have to worry about them the other days.

Answers: 1: No; 2: Yes; 3: Yes; 4: No

Problem-Solving

By now, you know there will be different types of obstacles and challenges on the path to growth mindset. One important skill to help achieve your dreams is problem-solving. In football, calling an audible is how the quarterback solves problems on the go without stopping and calling time-out. They call out strategies to their teammates in the middle of play. Problem-solving is coming up with new ways to improve skills, learn from mistakes, and find answers. When you are faced with a problem, follow these steps:

1. Identify the problem. You cannot problem-solve if you don't know what the problem is.

2. Brainstorm three possible solutions.

3. Identify the pros and cons of each possible solution.

4. Pick a solution and try it out.

Remember, if your first solution doesn't work, you can always try another one! Sometimes it takes a few attempts before you can successfully figure out a problem.

Along with a friend, create an obstacle course in your home or outside using cardboard, pillows, or paper. The goal is to make it to the opposite end of the course without passing through "lava," which is the ground around the objects you've laid out. Take turns completing the obstacle course. Remember, this is about strategy, so think: What's the easiest path? What's the quickest? Try to get to the other side with as few movements as possible. If you fall into the lava, consider what went wrong and strategize a new path to try.

Embracing Flexibility

To be a good problem-solver, embrace being flexible. Flexibility means you are able to change your plans, expectations, and approach without losing your nerve and giving up. Sometimes all you need to succeed is adaptability. This is the ability to adjust or modify a plan without fully changing it. If an adult was driving you to school and something happened to their car, you would adapt by finding another way to get to school. You could get on the bus rather than giving up because the original plan did not work.

Embrace flexibility by being curious. This will allow you to look at other options that could be even more useful. Don't become too attached to a single plan. Flexibility means the ability and willingness to switch it up. Change is not always easy, especially when you thought you had a great plan and suddenly you need to change course. Identify people who can help you when you may need to call an audible.

To play charades, you need at least two people. First, pick a subject. It could be famous movie characters, types of food, or anything else. The object of the game is to act out the name or thing without using words. Your teammate must guess the correct name. If your initial gesturing keeps falling to blank stares or incorrect guesses, adapt and try different movements. For added pressure, time each person's turn to one minute.

When you have finished a few rounds, reflect on how difficult it was for you to be flexible while your partner was guessing. Did it become easier or more difficult as you changed how you presented the word?

Celebrate Your Successes

Hug yourself tightly. You've made it to the end of the book, and you never gave up! There are some things that you will need to continue working on and practicing—have fun with this. You've done a marvelous job with the exercises, and you should be proud.

Making time to acknowledge your successes and hard work is important as you continue to develop your growth mindset. Acknowledge every milestone. This will encourage you to keep going. Celebrations don't have to be big or loud. A few words of praise and a fist bump in the mirror may be all you need. Feel free to share the news, too. Tell people who helped you along the way that you've reached your goal of finishing this book!

You've worked hard, so practice celebrating yourself! On the next page, create a certificate that honors your hard work. Include an affirmation, two major takeaways you want to remember, and the names of one to two people who you trust to always be in your corner. Draw a picture that symbolizes what finishing this book means to you. Be creative and colorful. You've earned this!

Dream Big!

You can do anything you want to do. All you need is the right attitude, people who support you, and a growth mindset. Remember to use all the resources from this book. Continue to motivate yourself with affirmations. Reframe unhelpful thoughts to kick negativity out of your way. Accept your flaws, and then work hard to turn them into strengths. Show yourself compassion when times get hard, and demonstrate empathy when you can relate to someone else's struggles. You are ready to take on the world and be your best self. You've got this!

GLOSSARY

affirmation: Positive statement that is repeated to help challenge negative thoughts

amygdala: The part of the brain connected to emotional memories

anxiety: Worry or unease about something

brain stem: The part of the brain that is responsible for things you do automatically, like your heartbeat, breathing, digesting food, and sneezing

cell: Smallest part in the structure of a living thing

cerebellum: The part of the brain that regulates muscular activity

cerebrum: The part of the brain that integrates sensory and neural functions with involuntary body activity

comfort zone: A place where you feel safe and in control

empathy: The ability to understand and be sensitive to the thoughts and experiences of others

Epsom salts: Colorless crystals that dissolve in water; they are said to have a calming effect on the body and encourage rest and relaxation

feedback: Information given to a person regarding their performance of a task

meditation: A mental exercise to train focus, attention, and awareness; mindfulness is one possible meditation technique

mindfulness: Being aware of and living in the present moment, not what happened in the past or what might happen in the future

neural pathways: Connections between brain cells that allow a person to learn new things

neurogenesis: The process of growing new neurons

neurons: Cells that work with the nervous system; they carry information throughout the human body

neuroplasticity: The brain's ability to change and grow throughout a person's life

nervous system: Consists of the brain, spinal cord, and nerves and controls everything a body does

perseverance: The ability to keep doing something even when it is difficult

prefrontal cortex: The part of the brain that controls choices, decisions, planning, and self-control

reframe: Express an idea in a different way

resilient: The ability to bounce back after challenges and difficult times

rumination: Going over something in the mind repeatedly

self-limiting belief: Stories we tell about ourselves that hold us back

self-talk: Conversations we have with ourselves

senses: Sight, smell, sound, taste, touch

spinal cord: A group of nerves that sends signals between the brain and other body parts

toxins: Harmful substances consisting mainly of protein

trigger: Something that evokes the memory of a harmful experience, creating an intense emotional reaction

visualize: Picture the outcome in your mind

vulnerable: Willing to show emotion or weakness

RESOURCES

Check out the following resources to learn more about growth mindset and keep developing your skills.

RESOURCES FOR KIDS

Growth Mindset Journal for Boys: A Space to Embrace Challenges, Set Goals, and Dream Big by Elizabeth Sautter and Gabriel Sautter Savala

This journal gives you further tools to develop a growth mindset for yourself. Through short writing prompts and simple activities, you'll continue to learn how to become stronger, braver, and happier just by changing the way you think.

DoSomething
dosomething.org

DoSomething.org is the largest nonprofit dedicated to youth and social change. Members join volunteer, social change, and civic action campaigns to make real-world impact on causes they care about.

Zero Hour
thisiszerohour.org

Zero Hour centers the voices of diverse youth in the conversation around climate and environmental justice.

RESOURCES FOR CAREGIVERS

MBK Alliance

obama.org/mbka

The MBK Alliance focuses on building safe, supportive communities for boys and young men of color where they have clear pathways to opportunity.

Mindful

mindful.org

A website dedicated to inspiring, guiding, and connecting anyone who wants to explore mindfulness, including kids.

Mindset Works

mindsetworks.com

The global leader in growth mindset, Mindset Works promotes a growth mindset through research, partnerships, programs for students and educators, other tools and resources, and advocacy. Founded by Carol Dweck, author of *Mindset: The New Psychology of Success*, and colleagues Dr. Lisa Blackwell and Eduardo Briceño.

VentureLab

venturelab.org

Founded by Cristal Glangchai, VentureLab empowers kids to innovate, create, and discover their potential.

youcubed

youcubed.org

Founded by Dr. Jo Boaler, youcubed brings growth mindset and mathematics together to inspire students with open, creative mindset mathematics.

REFERENCES

Boaler, Jo. *Limitless Mind: Learn, Lead, and Live Without Barriers.* New York: HarperOne, 2019.

"Brain Anatomy and How the Brain Works." Johns Hopkins Medicine. Accessed March 27, 2022. hopkinsmedicine.org /health/conditions-and-diseases/anatomy-of-the-brain.

Britannica. "Dreams from My Father: A Story of Race and Inheritance." Accessed March 25, 2022. britannica.com/topic /Dreams-from-My-Father-A-Story-of-Race-and-Inheritance.

Brown, Brené. *Braving the Wilderness: The Quest for True Belonging and the Courage to Stand Alone.* New York: Random House, 2017.

Casey, Nora Sørena. "Tyler Perry." Britannica. Last modified March 7, 2022. britannica.com/biography/Tyler-Perry.

Denworth, Lydia. "Debate Arises over Teaching 'Growth Mindsets' to Motivate Students." *Scientific American.* August 12, 2019. scientificamerican.com/article/debate-arises-over-teaching -growth-mindsets-to-motivate-students.

Duckworth, Angela. *Grit: The Power of Passion and Perseverance.* New York: Scribner, 2016.

Duncan, Arne. "The World's 100 Most Influential People: 2012." *Time*. April 18, 2012. content.time.com/time/specials/packages /article/0,28804,2111975_2111976_2111945,00.html.

Dweck, Carol. *Mindset: The New Psychology of Success*. New York: Ballantine Books, 2006.

Dzubow, Lauren. "The Secret to Obama's Success: He's Boring?" April 2009. oprah.com/money/what-makes-president-barack -obama-successful.

Editors of Biography.com. "Abraham Lincoln." February 12, 2018. biography.com/us-president/abraham-lincoln.

Editors of Encyclopedia Britannica. "Jay-Z." Accessed March 25, 2022. britannica.com/biography/Jay-Z.

Farson, Richard, and Ralph Keyes. "The Failure-Tolerant Leader." *Harvard Business Review*. August 2002. hbr.org/2002/08 /the-failure-tolerant-leader.

"Helping Kids Identify and Express Feelings." Kids Helpline. Accessed March 26, 2022. kidshelpline.com.au/parents/issues /helping-kids-identify-and-express-feelings.

History.com Editors. "Cesar Chavez." History.com. February 8, 2021. history.com/topics/mexico/cesar-chavez.

Intellectual Ventures. "Failing for Success: Thomas Edison." January 26, 2016. intellectualventures.com/buzz/insights /failing-for-success-thomas-edison.

Jeremy Lin Foundation. Accessed March 25, 2022. jeremylinfoundation.org.

Lloyd, Rees. "Lessons from the Life of a Great American." *Record Gazette*. March 29, 2007. recordgazette.net/news/lessons-from -the-life-of-a-great-american-cesar-chavez/article_8505a9c9-77c0 -5cbe-a69e-b1ecdfed8724.html.

"Mistakes Grow Your Brain." youcubed. youcubed.org/evidence /mistakes-grow-brain.

Pawel, Miriam. "How Cesar Chavez Changed the World." *Smith-sonian Magazine*. November 2013. smithsonianmag.com/history /how-cesar-chavez-changed-the-world-3735853.

Russo Bullaro, Grace. "The Incredible World of Child Activists: They're Scared, but Want to Save the World." *VNY Media La Voce di New York*. February 10, 2021. lavocedinewyork.com/en /news/2021/02/10/the-incredible-world-of-child-activists -theyre-scared-but-want-to-save-the-world.

Scharneberg, Kirsten, and Kim Barker. "The Not-So-Simple Story of Barack Obama's Youth." *Chicago Tribune*. March 25, 2007. chicagotribune.com/chi-070325obama-youth-story-archive -story.html.

Washington Post Staff and Contributors. "12 Kids Who Are Changing Their Communities and Our World." *Washington Post*. April 11, 2020. washingtonpost.com/kidspost/2020/04/11/12-kids-who -are-changing-their-communities-our-world.

INDEX

Self-compassion, 73, 118

Self-limiting beliefs, 45

Self-portrait, 126

Self-talk, 42–44, 65

Self-worth, 125

Senses, 38

Sleep, 29, 33

Spinal cord, 22

Strengths, 12–13

Successes, celebrating, 67, 135–137

Success planning, 88

Superpowers, 12–13

T

Talking it out, 110–111

Thought records, 49

Thoughts, 36. *See also* Reframing
    thoughts; Unhelpful thoughts

Toxins, 29

Triggers, 49

U

Uncertainty, 55–56, 59

Unhelpful thoughts, 45, 61

V

Vision boards, 10–11

Visualization, 14, 56

Vitamin D, 26

Vulnerability, 111

W

Water, drinking, 29

Wins, celebrating, 67, 135–137

Worry cycles, 66

Y

"Yet," power of, 87–88

Acknowledgments

My parents have always encouraged me to pursue my passion, no matter the obstacles. Dunni, all I ever want is for you to be proud to call me your big bro. To my partner, you bring nothing but Joi into my life—cheers to forever. To my chosen family, Suede, Steph, Maris, Tee, Mandy, Gin, Daj, Toolie, Alexanders, Polo, Davey, Nesh—thank you. You all motivate me more than I can ever express.

About the Author

Oluwatosin "Tosin" Akindele is passionate about working with youth. Tosin has worked with kids in foster care, high school, and elementary school. As a therapist, he works primarily with boys and men through a private practice in New York. One thing he has carried from his experiences is the power of believing in yourself and using your own strengths to improve all areas of your life. Follow Tosin on Instagram at @therapy4usbyus and learn more about him at TherapyForUsByUs.com.